A Note to Parents

DK READERS is a compelling new program for beginning readers, designed in conjunction with leading literacy experts, including Dr. Linda Gambrell, Director of the School of Education at Clemson University. Dr. Gambrell has served on the Board of Directors of the International Reading Association and as President of the National Reading Conference.

Beautiful illustrations and superb full-color photographs combine with engaging, easy-to-read stories to offer a fresh approach to each subject in the series. Each DK READER is guaranteed to capture a child's interest while developing his or her reading skills, general knowledge, and love of reading.

The four levels of DK READERS are aimed at different reading abilities, enabling you to choose the books that are exactly right for your child:

Level 1 – Beginning to read
Level 2 – Beginning to read alone
Level 3 – Reading alone
Level 4 – Proficient readers

The "normal" age at which a child begins to read can be anywhere from three to eight years old, so these levels are intended only as a general guideline.

No matter which level you select, you can be sure that you are helping your child learn to read, then read to learn!

Project Editors Penny Smith,
Caroline Bingham, and Mary Atkinson
Designer Michelle Baxter
Senior Editor Linda Esposito
Deputy Managing Art Editor
Jane Horne
US Editor Regina Kahney
Production Kate Oliver
Picture Researcher Catherine Edkins
Illustrator Peter Dennis

Reading Consultant
Linda B. Gambrell, Ph.D.

First American edition. 1998
12 13 14 15 16 17 18 19 25 24 23 22 21
Published in the United States by
DK Publishing, Inc.
375 Hudson Street, New York, New York 10014
025-KP800-Jun/1998

Published in Great Britain by Dorling Kindersley Limited.

Library of Congress Cataloging-in-Publication Data
Maynard, Christopher
Days of The Knights / by Christopher Maynard -- 1st American ed.
p.   cm. -- (Eyewitness readers. Level 4)
ISBN-13: 978-0-7894-2963-6
1. Knights and knighthood--Juvenile literature. 2. Civilization,
Medieval -- Juvenile literature. [1. Knight and knighthood.
2. Civilization, Medieval.] I. DK Publishing, Inc. II. Series.
CR4513.K53   1998
940.1--DC21
                                                97-29396
                                                CIP
                                                AC
Color reproduction by Colourscan
Printed and bound in China by L Rex Printing Co., Ltd

The publisher would like to thank the following
for their kind permission to reproduce their photographs:
c=center; t=top; b=below; l=left; r=right

Ancient, Art and Architecture: Ronald Sheridan 5cr; 10tl, 27br; **AKG,
London:** 29cr; **Board of Trustees of the Armouries:** 21br; **Bridgeman
Art Library, London:** Biblioteca Estense, Modena 16tl; Bibliotheque de
L'Arsenal, Paris 37tr; British Library 6tl, 10cl, 14bl, 27tr, 35tr;
Bibliotheque Nationale, Paris 3c, 6cl, 9tr; Ecole des Beaux Arts, Paris,
Giraudon 30cl; Fitzwilliam Museum, University of Cambridge 26bc;
Musee Conde, Chantilly, France, Giraudon 36b; Victoria & Albert
Museum, London 32tl; **British Museum, London:** 39tr; **English
Heritage:** 32bl, 38br, 46bl; Ivan Lapper 46tl; **ETArchive:** 29tr, 38tl;
Bibliotheque Nationale, Paris 5tr; **Mary Evans Picture Library:**
14tl,16cl, 23cr, 38cl; Explorer 24bl; Institution of Civil Engineers 1br,
20tr, 47cl; **Robert Harding Picture Library:** British Library 24tl, 40b;
The Marsden Archive: Simon Marsden 45tr; **Museum of London:** 39cr,
43cr; **Wallace Collection:** 20l, 21cr, 47tr;

Jacket: **ET Archive:** Bibliotheque Nationale, Paris front main image;
Wallace Collection: front cr

Additional photography by Geoff Brightling, Geoff Dann,
Mike Dunning, Dave King, Tim Ridley, and Jerry Young.

Contents

DAYS OF THE KNIGHTS

A TALE OF CASTLES AND BATTLES

Written by Christopher Maynard

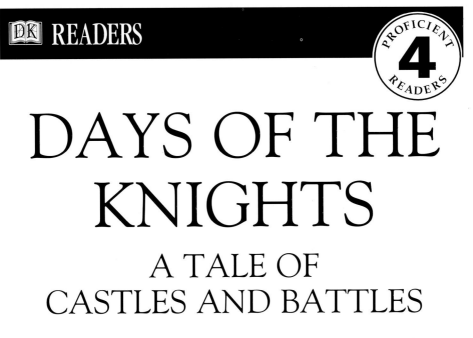

DK Publishing, Inc.

Under attack!

The creak of wagon wheels broke the early-morning silence. Then the watchmen spotted dark shapes in the mist. Suddenly, the castle guards understood.

"We're under attack!" they cried.

Enemy soldiers had reached the castle before the guards knew what was happening. They were taking the mighty fortress by surprise, just as the baron had planned!

For years, the baron and Henry, the lord of the castle, had been enemies. Lately Lord Henry had built up his castle's defenses. The baron took this as a bad sign, and he decided to attack.

The castle soldiers knew what to do. They bolted the gate and pulled up the heavy drawbridge. Then they raced to the battlements – the jagged tops of the castle walls. From there, they could fire their longbows and crossbows, and drop rocks on enemy soldiers who tried to scale the walls.

Down below, the baron's soldiers jeered and shouted at the men on the battlements. The enemy had quickly surrounded the castle. There was no escape!

Battlements
These are at the tops of the castle walls. The gaps are called crenels.

Drawbridge
This bridge could be lifted up to cover the castle entrance. Some drawbridges had trapdoors leading to a deep pit!

5

Garrison
The soldiers who defended a castle were either noble-born knights or hired men.

Siege camp
The enemy set up a siege camp outside the castle because it might take months for the castle to fall.

Meanwhile, other enemy soldiers started looting the nearby village. They stole beds, chairs, and food from houses. They broke into barns and took pigs and chickens.

Then they set fire to bundles of straw and threw them into the wooden buildings. Terrified villagers rushed screaming from their blazing homes.

The soldiers of the castle garrison saw the flames. They heard the cries of the villagers. Many of the soldiers had friends in the village. But there was nothing they could do. They were trapped behind the castle walls.

As smoke filled the air, a train of ox carts rumbled up to the castle. The baron's soldiers began to unpack tents, food, and weapons. They were setting up a siege camp – a temporary village to live in while they starved out the people in the castle. They had to be well prepared.

Catapult
Besides firing rocks, catapults were used to send dead animals over the castle walls. This was a good way to spread disease!

The baron sent word to Lord Henry. His message was short and clear. "Surrender now, or die later!"

Lord Henry's answer was just as clear. "Never!" he declared.

Furious, the baron gave a signal, and the long siege began. Huge catapults clanged, flinging boulders at the walls. A round of flaming arrows sailed over the battlements. Some of the attackers dumped logs and soil into the moat – a water-filled ditch around the castle. Soon the moat would be full enough to walk across.

From the castle, archers kept up a deadly shower of arrows, firing through narrow slits in the castle walls. Other soldiers showered rocks and boiling oil on the enemy below.

Near the castle walls, a band of attackers inched forward with a siege tower. This tower was a giant stairway that could hold hundreds of soldiers. Soon the high battlements would be under attack!

Amazingly, the castle held out for weeks. The baron could not find a way to break through the walls. But the castle garrison was in terrible shape. There was no fresh meat, because all the animals had been eaten. Even rats were getting hard to find. Most days the soldiers ate only a handful of oats. They could not last much longer.

Bows
The bow, a vital part of an archer's equipment, cost almost a week's pay.

Siege tower
When this tower was wheeled up to the castle walls, hundreds of attacking soldiers could climb up into the castle.

Bombard
This weapon fired huge stone cannonballs that could smash down the walls of a castle.

Hostages
Important prisoners were taken to the enemy's castle. Here they could sometimes roam until money was paid for their release.

Finally the attackers dragged up a huge cannon, called a bombard. The sight of it filled the garrison with despair. They knew that the castle was finished.

Late that night, a band of men sneaked out of the castle. They fell to their knees in front of the enemy soldiers and begged to be taken to the baron.

"Get my men into the castle and I will spare your lives," said the baron.

The traitors led a small party of enemy knights to a secret entrance. Under the cover of darkness, the attackers slipped into the castle and opened the gates.

The baron's army rushed in, and the mighty castle was soon taken.

From tower to dungeon, the soldiers swept through, looting anything they could find. They killed Lord Henry and his wife and took the rest of his family as hostages. But in the confusion, one person slipped out the secret door. It was the castle nursemaid. In her arms she held a small child – the lord's son, Thomas. ❖

Looting
Gold, silver, jewelry, and clothing were carried off by looters. They also took away money that the lord had collected for taxes.

Fairs
Small fairs lasted a few days. Bigger ones might run for a week.

Merchants
These men traveled to faraway places and brought back fine goods to sell, such as cloth, glassware, and unusual spices.

Fairs and holy days

"Look there!" Little Thomas tugged on his nurse's skirt. "That man's standing on his hands!"

Thomas was a young boy now. Since the siege, he had been living at his uncle's castle. Today he was excited because the nearby village was having a fair for the feast of St. Dunstan. There was a lot to see!

Merchants and traders called out to the crowds. From their stalls they were selling everything from honey to herring. Thomas's nurse was hoping a merchant would turn up with some fine cloth. There! She could see some.

Thomas didn't care about cloth. He liked to watch the dancing bears and the jugglers.

Mummers
These traveling actors often put on religious plays.

Ale
Poor villagers drank ale, which was like beer. Wine was more expensive.

When Thomas got back to his uncle's castle that afternoon, the whole place buzzed with excitement, and everyone joined in the fun. No work would be done today!

A band of traveling actors, called mummers, had arrived the night before. Today, in the castle courtyard, they were staging the tragic tale of Noah and the Great Flood. The play was complete with fancy costumes, songs, and sound effects.

A group of children wriggled through the crowd that had gathered to watch. "Let me through!" shouted Thomas. "I can't see anything!"

Thomas's uncle called to one of his servants. The servant hurried to bring a few barrels of wine and plenty of ale for the guests to drink.

Pouring wine at festival time

Soon the chatter of the guests was even louder than the actors' voices. "Speak up!" the crowd shouted.

Adding to the noise, a troop of acrobats began to perform. They shouted to the crowd to watch their tumbling tricks.

Later, when the sun had set, traveling musicians, called minstrels, entertained Thomas's uncle and his guests. They sang songs and told stories of faraway battles and famous heroes. This was Thomas's favorite part of the day. ❖

Minstrels
Wandering musicians were a good source of news and gossip, as well as music!

A minstrel playing a hornpipe

15

Page
A page was taught polite manners and how to use a sword.

Squire
His job was to look after a knight's armor and weapons.

Dubbing
After a tap on the shoulder with a sword, a squire became a knight.

Knight school

"Attack, men!" Thomas yelled. At his signal, the young soldiers rushed across the courtyard and stormed into the great hall. But no one took notice – Thomas and his soldiers were only six years old!

But when Thomas was seven, everything changed. He left his uncle's castle to live with another noble family. There he worked as a page. This was the first step to becoming a knight.

As a page, Thomas learned to ride and fight. He was lucky – he was also taught to read and write.

When he turned 14, Thomas became a squire. He served a knight and followed him everywhere – once even into battle!

By the time he was 20, Thomas had proved that he was a fit and worthy man. Finally, in a special ceremony, he was dubbed a knight. ❖

Fastening armor
Each piece of armor was tied in place with long leather straps.

Dressed to kill

"Sir Thomas, please stand still," grunted the squire. He braced his foot on the knight's back and tugged on the leather straps.

"Sorry, Roger," Thomas said. Usually he was more helpful putting on the armor. But today his thoughts were somewhere else. Today was the tournament!

"Roger, do you think Lady Elaine will be watching?" Thomas asked.

The squire rolled his eyes. "Probably, sir," he answered. "But if you don't hurry, sir, you may miss the tournament – and Lady Elaine!"

Roger had already strapped four pieces of armor to each of Thomas's legs. He was struggling with the breastplate and backplate when his master held up one hand. "Just a moment, Roger. I have an itch."

Roger looked like he wanted to thump his master. Instead he scratched the itch, then went back to his task, strapping on the arm and shoulder pieces.

Then Roger handed Thomas his gauntlets and stepped back. Truly, thought Roger, a knight in shining armor was a splendid sight!

Helmet

Breastplate

Gauntlet (metal glove)

Spur

Armor
A good suit of armor could cost a knight as much as a new car costs today.

Swords
These could
be twice the
length of a
man's arm
and as heavy
as a bicycle.

Thomas's suit of armor was a gift from his uncle. It was made of the finest German steel but had been in the family for many years and was dented all over. Thomas did not have the money to pay an armor-maker to hammer out the dents. His squire did his best to shine the steel and keep off the rust. But Thomas still felt a little ashamed.

Even worse than the well-worn armor was the condition of Thomas's weapons. His shield was dented and had long, deep scratches running across it. His lance, a long spear, was brightly painted, but in some places the paint had started to chip.

His razor-sharp sword was his one treasure. It had belonged to his father and was found after the siege.

His uncle had kept the sword until Thomas was knighted. It had a fine silver handle and was still a thing of great beauty. Thomas wished he could afford to have the dents and scrapes on its surface fixed.

Today his luck could change. If Thomas could knock another knight off his horse, he would win that knight's valuable horse and armor.

"The first money I get will go toward a new set of weapons," Thomas told Roger. "I'll buy a nice heavy mace and order a complete repair job for my sword."

A tournament was only one way to earn money. Battles were another. In the next battle, Thomas promised himself, he would make sure he got a large share of the looted goods.

Shield
This leather-covered shield has a curved edge where a lance could be rested.

Mace
The knobby metal end of this war club could easily break bones. Maces were used mostly in foot combat.

Horse armor

Horses were dressed in full armor for battle, but for a tournament only their heads were protected. This metal face armor was called a shaffron.

Jousts

One popular tournament event was the joust. Knights on horseback charged each other with long lances.

When Thomas was ready, he made his way to the tournament field. The sight of Lady Elaine took his mind off his worries.

He stood with her as the mock battles began. Together they watched important knights charge across the field on their horses.

Two knights competing in a joust

The faces of the knights were hidden by helmets, but Thomas knew each knight by the colors he wore.

Over his armor, each knight wore a tunic sewn with the crest or emblem that belonged to his family. The knights' horses were also draped in cloths in the family colors.

Helmets
Jousting helmets were three times heavier than war helmets.

Coat of arms
The crest and colors of a family were known as its coat of arms. This was passed down from father to oldest son.

Water jousts
Sometimes knights jousted from boats. Jousting lances were made from hollow wood that would shatter and do less harm than solid lances.

How to win
Knocking a knight out of his saddle was an outright win. A knight also won points for breaking his lance on a rival's shield.

Tournaments were fun for the knights, but they had a serious purpose as well. The knights used the mock battles as practice for the real thing.

At each end of the castle field, dozens of knights on horseback waited for the chance to joust. Soon it was Thomas's turn. At the signal, he galloped toward the other knight with his lance lowered, aiming for the center of the man's shield. If he hit it hard enough and in just the right place, he would knock the knight to the ground.

There was a thunder of hooves and the crack of splintering wood as both lances shattered. With a grunt of pain, the other knight toppled from his saddle. He landed and quickly rolled out of the way.

Thomas was concerned until he saw that the man was not hurt.

Then Thomas smiled.
He'd done it. He'd won the
joust – and a new
set of armor!
His eyes swept
over the crowd.
There, smiling
back, was
Lady Elaine. ❖

Estate
All of a lord's lands, even when they were spread far across the country, were part of his estate.

Build it strong

"Great bones!" Lord Thomas exclaimed. "At last the king has granted me permission to build a castle!" He let out a whoop of delight.

A writ
Writs were drawn up to grant the king's permission for land or hunting rights.

The royal seal makes the writ official.

Thomas had become a lord and married Lady Elaine. He had spent many years as a knight in loyal service to the king, winning great riches in battle, as well as the king's respect. Several years before, the king had given Thomas a large piece of land. Now, finally, he had said that Thomas could build a home there.

Building the castle would take ten years or more – if the money held out. Even just planning a castle was a huge task.

First Thomas had to hire a master mason – an expert to design the castle and oversee the building of it. He chose a well-respected mason named Master James.

Together they picked the spot for the castle – a high point that formed a natural defense against attacks. A nearby river would provide a source of clean drinking water within the castle walls in case of a siege.

Lord
A lord also acted as a local judge. He settled any disputes among the people living on his land.

Master mason
Master masons traveled the countryside, working on several castles at a time.

Only wealthy people had proper beds. The very rich had feather mattresses; most mattresses were made of woven straw.

Lord Thomas was too young to remember the siege on his father's castle. But his nurse had told him all about it, so he was determined to make his fortress strong enough to withstand attacks.

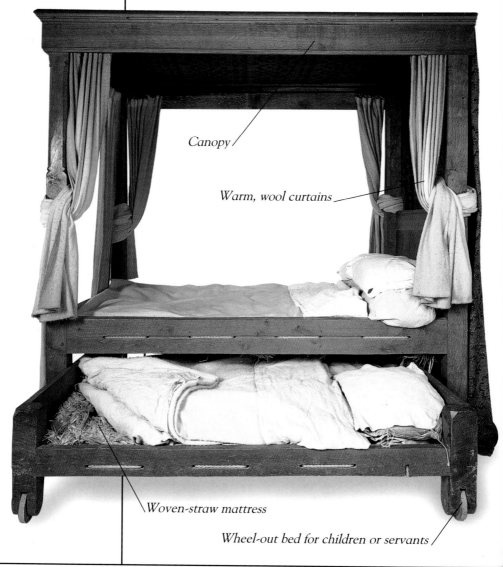

Canopy

Warm, wool curtains

Woven-straw mattress

Wheel-out bed for children or servants

Thomas also wanted a castle where he could invite important guests. Traveling was difficult and dangerous, so visitors often stayed for weeks. They would need splendid rooms in which they could relax and sleep in comfort.

And Thomas wanted a great hall for entertaining. He planned to hold lots of concerts and feasts!

Above all, the castle had to be a comfortable home for his family, his knights, and his servants. Plans would include private rooms for his wife and children, a well-stocked wine cellar, and a huge kitchen.

Of course, there would also be a chapel where a priest would say prayers and bless Thomas's family each day.

These days, Lord Thomas had a lot to be thankful for.

Knight
Knights helped their lords keep control over their lands.

Chapel
A lord would have a small family chapel near his rooms and a bigger one in the courtyard for his servants.

Moat
A moat was a good defense during an attack. It was also a great place to fish!

Artisans
Skilled workers such as carpenters and stonemasons spent many years learning their trades. Stonemasons were the most highly paid of all artisans.

"Master James, you are a marvel," said Lord Thomas as he looked over the plans for the new castle. "This is exactly what I had in mind. But please make sure it is as strong as possible. The walls must be at least ten feet (three meters) thick, and we need to add a great moat all around the outside. It must be very deep."

Master James nodded. From then on, he was in charge. He arranged for a mountain of stone, wood, and other building materials to be brought to the site. He also hired workers from the nearby villages.

Some of the workers were stonemasons, who would cut and carve blocks of stone. Other workers would build the castle walls. Master James brought in carpenters to put up scaffolding – a wooden frame around the castle for the workers to stand on while they worked high above the ground.

He sent for blacksmiths to make and repair tools. He hired men to dig ditches and wells, and to carry heavy loads.

The army of workers would toil from dawn to dusk, building the castle by hand with saws, axes, chisels, and mallets. ❖

Tools
The tools used to build a castle were similar to many tools used today.

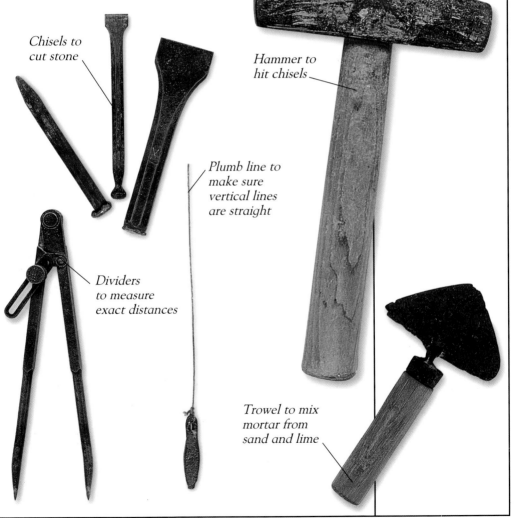

Chisels to cut stone

Hammer to hit chisels

Plumb line to make sure vertical lines are straight

Dividers to measure exact distances

Trowel to mix mortar from sand and lime

Gatehouse
Sometimes rich prisoners were kept in the gatehouse. Poor ones died in dungeons.

Murder holes
These were holes in the ceiling behind the portcullis. Archers would fire arrows at attackers through these small gaps.

On guard!

While the castle was being built, Lord Thomas made a few changes. He worried constantly about an attack. With so many people living and working within the castle walls, he would not sleep well unless he knew the castle was as strong as possible.

He ordered Master James to put up a gatehouse. This huge stone building would protect the entrance.

Inside the gateway, the masons placed an extra-strong oak and iron gate called a portcullis. It was so heavy that it took two men and special winding gear to budge it.

At the same time, other workers put up wooden scaffolding and built a tall stone tower. Its walls were several feet (meters) thick. This would be a safe place for Lord Thomas and his family to live in times of trouble.

After many years the castle was finally finished. Inside its walls was a courtyard with workshops for tailors, candlemakers, carpenters, and potters. Peasants came to buy things they needed. Peddlers came to sell small items like brushes and ribbons.

Lord Thomas wanted the castle to be a safe place to do business. To keep out pickpockets and thieves, he posted sentries at the gate. They stopped people and searched their packs before letting them inside.

"Hey! You with the sack! Let's see what you've got!" a sentry called to a peddler he didn't know. The peddler tried to slip the guard a coin, but he was turned away. This guard was honest – he would not be bribed.

At the end of each day, a bell rang out and everyone went home. The gates were pulled closed. But the guards stayed on duty all night. ❖

Peasants
These people were virtual slaves to the lord. They worked on his land and, in return, could grow crops to feed themselves.

It took weeks
to prepare for
a visit from a
king. Nearly
a hundred
people would
come along
with him.

The visitor

The royal messenger clattered into the courtyard. He pulled his tired horse to a stop and sprang to the ground. A guard led him into the great hall, where he gave his message to Lord Thomas.

Thomas's eyebrows lifted in surprise as he read the letter. Quickly he wrote out a short answer and handed it to the messenger.

A king and his nobles riding toward a castle

Then he turned to Lady Elaine. "We are going to have a visitor," he said. "The king is coming to stay!"

So many things needed to be done to get ready for a royal visit. The first task was to order new clothes. There were no clothing stores back then, so Lord Thomas and Lady Elaine called in a tailor to make their clothes. The tailor would sew every stitch by hand.

Thomas wanted a short robe with fur-trimmed sleeves. He also ordered the latest style hat, the kind that sat high on the head. Lady Elaine had her heart set on a dress with a long train to flow behind her as she walked, and a hat to match.

Once his wardrobe was taken care of, Thomas turned his thoughts to entertainment. During the day there would be hunting and hawking for his guests, and at night they would enjoy music and feasts.

Clothing
Rich people wore costly fabrics. Clothes were sometimes stored in smelly toilets to keep away moths.

Overshoes
Wooden platforms, called pattens, were worn under shoes to keep them out of the mud.

Courtiers
These officials served the king at court and during visits.

East tower
Rooms built in towers were the easiest to defend.

Kitchen
This was often built in the courtyard because of the risk of fire.

Lady Elaine got busy arranging the king's living quarters. The east tower was always kept free for important visitors. With its three floors of comfortable rooms set apart from the rest of the castle, it would be safe and private for the king.

Next came the important job of deciding what they should feed the king and the dozens of courtiers and other officials who would be traveling with him.

A castle kitchen

Lady Elaine had several meetings with the cook. The kitchen would soon be very busy.

The cook began by ordering supplies. Great sides of beef and bacon, barrels of pickled vegetables, and strings of onions soon filled the pantry. Sacks of wholewheat flour stood ready to be baked into bread. Tubs of honey to sweeten drinks and food were stacked three high.

Down in the cellar, the steward checked the wine barrels to make sure the wine was fit to drink.

The cook checked his supply of pots, sharpened his knives, and then set to work planning his menus. He could count on a supply of fish from the castle moat. Fruits and herbs would be picked from the castle gardens. And once the guests arrived, fresh meat would be brought back by the hunting parties. There would be feasts every day!

Pots and pans
Cooking was done over fires. This cauldron hung by chains over the heat.

Carving knife
Sharp knives were needed to cut up animals killed by hunting parties.

Fish
This was eaten fresh, or it was salted to keep it from rotting.

Hunting dogs
Packs of dogs
were trained to
track prey by
scent. When
cornered, boars
tried to escape
by stabbing the
dogs with their
sharp tusks.

Deer hunting
Hunting deer
helped train
young knights
for war. They
rode swift
hunting horses
called coursers.

Finally, one sunny morning, the king and his party rode up to the castle gates.

The king loved to hunt – he had brought his own pack of hunting dogs. At the first opportunity, Lord Thomas took him to the forest with a party of knights and lords. They rode Thomas's best hunting horses. "I saw deer by the stream earlier, my lord," said the gamekeeper.

A royal hunter and his pack of dogs chasing a deer

The dogs soon picked up the scent and flushed out the deer. Then the hunting party came across the trail of a wild pig, called a boar. After battling the entire dog pack, the boar ran into a dense thicket where the dogs couldn't get at it. Finally two knights on foot killed it with their spears.

Later that day the king and Lord Thomas went hawking. They used Thomas's trained hawks and falcons to catch rabbits and small birds. Servants took the animals back to the castle for the feast. Lord Thomas was proud to serve his guests with food that came from his own land.

Hawking
Prized birds of prey were kept in a building called a mews or in a lord's rooms.

Wild boar
Served with apples, boar was a regular after-hunt dish.

The nobles began their feast by merrily raising their goblets. "To the king!" they shouted.

Servants carried in metal plates, heaped high with roasted pheasant, boar, and deer.

Pheasants
Feathers were pushed back into cooked pheasants to make them look lifelike.

At the table
Diners had their own silverware, but often shared cups.

Next came huge bowls filled to the brim with fruit and nuts. There was even a ship made of spun sugar.

As music floated from the minstrel gallery, Thomas and his guests feasted happily far into the night. ❖

Bread plates
Servants ate off stale bread, which soaked up gravy and could be eaten after the meat.

Wine
Castle residents drank lots of wine. At one castle, in 1370, soldiers were paid in wine – they got 5 pints (3 liters) for a day's work.

Early castles

The first castles were built in the 900s. They were made of earth and lumber.

Bodiam Castle

This English castle is about 600 years old. The wealthy owner had seven halls built within its walls.

Old stones

The great hall is silent now. No one is cooking in the castle kitchen. No one is hunting wild boar in the forest. There are no knights left to joust. The castle is in ruins.

By the end of the 1400s, when cannons and bombards were able to destroy stone walls, many lords had left their castles. They moved into smaller, more comfortable homes.

Some castles stayed in good shape. Some were repaired after many years. And some castles had people living in them all that time. In a few castles, these were the descendants of the original owners.

But in many places, when the lords left, their castles fell to ruins. People took the lumber and helped themselves to the stones. The castles were battered by the weather.

Castle ghost
Years ago a butler hanged himself in one of this Irish castle's towers. His ghostly figure is said to walk the castle today.

Beeston Castle
This English castle was built high on a rocky summit over 700 years ago.

Beeston today
The castle is now in ruins. The footbridge crosses a ditch cut from solid rock!

Visitors still come to the castles. But they wear blue jeans and T-shirts instead of fur-trimmed robes. They carry cameras rather than swords and lances. They do not come for a feast – they come to learn. What can they discover from a bunch of old stones?

Castle ruins can tell fascinating stories about how people once lived. A large gatehouse and thick, strong battlements show that a castle was likely to be subjected to long attacks by enemy lords. Arrow slits and murder holes are clues that the castle residents were ready to defend themselves.

Castle walls also speak to us. Some have the outlines of old fireplaces. These outlines show us the rooms where people lived, ate, and slept.

Experts dig up the ground around a castle looking for things from the past. Next to some castles, they may find the remains of a garbage pit. Back then, all the castle trash was dumped into a large ditch.

The garbage gives us a vivid picture of life in castle times. Animal

bones show what people ate. Old coins give dates for kings and queens. If the searchers are lucky, they might find a knight's sword, helmet, or shield.

If you visit a castle, take time to imagine what life was like in its heyday. Think about the excitement of a joust, the unusual food, the damp dungeons, and the traitors who may have walked within its walls. Have fun making up stories about its past! ❖

Decorative old coins
These show important people and events from the past.

Staircases
These almost always turned to the right, so when an attacker tried to climb the stairs, he had no space to swing his sword.

Glossary

Artisans
Skilled craftsmen such as carpenters, metalworkers, and stonemasons.

Battlements
The tops of castle walls where soldiers can fire on attackers.

Bombard
A cannon that fires huge stone cannonballs.

Catapult
A machine for hurling large rocks.

Coat of arms
The symbols and colors displayed by a noble family on their battle equipment.

Courtiers
Officials and nobles who serve the king at court.

Drawbridge
A bridge that can be raised and lowered.

Dubbing
Ceremony in which a king or queen taps a squire on the shoulder with a sword to make him a knight.

Estate
The total of all a lord's lands and properties.

Garrison
The soldiers assigned to defend a castle.

Gatehouse
A huge tower that surrounds the main gate.

Gauntlets
Metal gloves that are worn as part of a suit of armor.

Hostages
Prisoners who are sent back to their friends and families in return for payment.

Joust
A competition between two knights in which each tries to knock the other off his horse.

Lance
A very long, swordlike weapon with a pointed tip.

Looters
Attackers who take away things of value from castles or other buildings.

Lord
A nobleman or knight who owns land providing food for his family and servants.

Mace
A club with a metal end that can break bones.

Master mason
A skilled craftsman who designs a castle.

Minstrels
Wandering musicians who sing and play to entertain the court.

Moat
A large, water-filled ditch that surrounds a castle to protect it.

Mummers
A troupe of traveling actors who put on plays.

Page
A noble boy in the first stage of training for knighthood.

Peasants
People who work on a lord's land in return for growing crops to feed themselves.

Peddler
A traveling salesman who sells small items.

Scaffolding
A temporary wooden framework around a building.

Sentry
A soldier who guards part of a castle and stops strangers from entering.

Siege camp
A temporary village where attackers live while they starve out a castle's inhabitants.

Siege tower
A huge, covered stairway that can be wheeled up to a castle's walls.

Squire
A teenage boy who is training to be a knight.

Writ
An official document granting permission or passing a law.

Index

Slashing swords, shining
armor, knights locked
in deadly battle – the
mighty castle is under siege!

DK READERS

Stunning photographs combine with lively
illustrations and engaging, age-appropriate stories in
DK READERS, a multilevel reading program guaranteed
to capture children's interest while developing
their reading skills and general knowledge.

1 BEGINNING TO READ	Beginning to read	• Word repetition, limited vocabulary, and simple sentences • Picture dictionary boxes
2 BEGINNING TO READ ALONE	Beginning to read alone	• Longer sentences and increased vocabulary • Information boxes full of extra fun facts • Simple index
3 READING ALONE	Reading alone	• More complex sentence structure • Information boxes and alphabetical glossary • Comprehensive index
4 PROFICIENT READERS	Proficient readers	• Rich vocabulary and challenging sentence structure • Additional information and alphabetical glossary • Comprehensive index

With DK READERS,
children will le_____d –
then rea___

$3.99 USA
$4.99 Canada

See our complete product line at
www.dk.com

ISBN 978-0-7894-2963-6   Printed in China

9 780789 429636

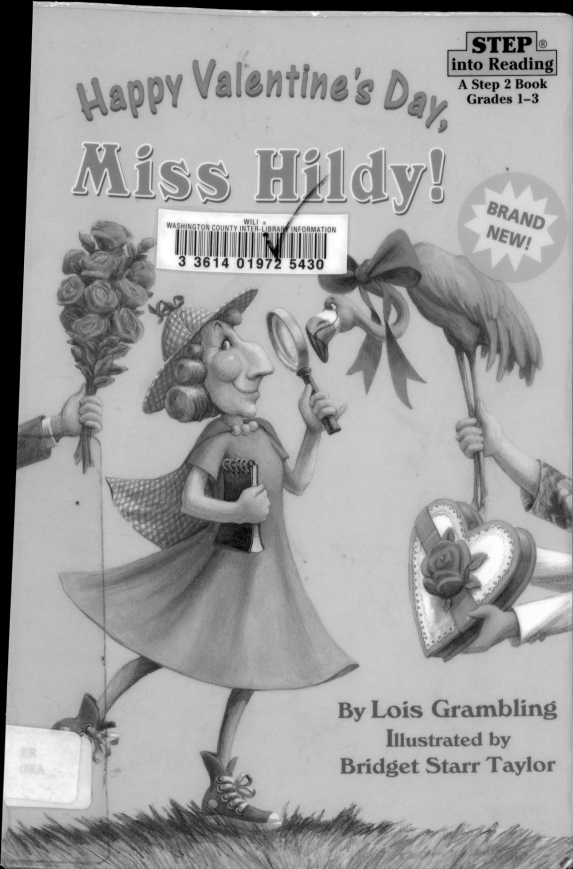

Happy Valentine's Day,
Miss Hildy!

BRAND
NEW!

By Lois Grambling

Illustrated by
Bridget Starr Taylor

I have read this book all by myself!

_____

(my name)

_____

(date)